DESPEGUE / DEPARTURE

Víctor Rodríguez Núñez (Havana, 1955) is one of Cuba's most outstanding and celebrated contemporary writers, with over eighty collections of his poetry published throughout the world. He has been the recipient of major awards in the Spanish-speaking region. His selected poems have been translated into over a dozen languages and he has read his poetry in over fifty countries. He divides his time between Gambier, Ohio, where he is Professor of Spanish at Kenyon College, and Havana, Cuba. www.victorrodrigueznunez.com

Katherine M. Hedeen is a prize-winning translator of poetry and an essayist. Her latest translations include collections by Juan Calzadilla, Antonio Gamoneda, Fina García Marruz, and Raúl Gómez Jattin. She is the co-editor, with Welsh poet Zoë Skoulding, of the groundbreaking transatlantic translation anthology, *Poetry's Geographies* (Eulalia / Shearsman 2022). She is Managing Editor of Action Books. She resides in Ohio, where she is Professor of Spanish at Kenyon College, and Havana, Cuba. www.katherinemhedeen.com

a la memoria de Alberto Rodríguez Tosca

in memory of Alberto Rodríguez Tosca

© 2016 poems: Víctor Rodríguez Núñez. © 2024 translation: Katherine M. Hedeen. All rights reserved; no part of this book may be reproduced by any means without the publisher's permission.

ISBN: 978-1-916938-25-0

The author has asserted their right to be identified as the author of this Work in accordance with the Copyright, Designs and Patents Act 1988

Cover art by Tonel (Antonio Eligio Fernández)

Edited & typeset by Aaron Kent

Broken Sleep Books Ltd
Rhydwen
Talgarreg
Ceredigion
SA44 4HB

Broken Sleep Books Ltd
Fair View
St Georges Road
Cornwall
PL26 7YH

CONTENTS

IV. PUERTO / IV. PORT

V. ENTRADA / V. ENTRANCE

despegue / departure

Víctor Rodríguez Núñez
Translated by Katherine M. Hedeen

Broken Sleep Books

El alma despegada contempla
las partes de sí que no partieron
— Juan Gelman

the soul departed contemplates
the parts of itself that did not part
— Juan Gelman

TO BE HERE AND EVERYWHERE:
Víctor Rodríguez Núñez's *departure*

The soul departed contemplates
the parts of itself that did not part

These verses by the Argentine poet Juan Gelman (1930-2014) haunt Cuban poet Víctor Rodríguez Núñez's prize-winning *despegue* / *departure*.[1] Gelman's poetry is infinitely experimental, plays at the dismantling of words. Here is no exception. In English, the word *despegue* can mean "unstuck," "detach," "peel off" as in when the glue stops working; "takeoff" as in an airplane; "start" as in the beginning of something, "come apart" as in break, or "leave" as in separate from. Such variations are no doubt why Rodríguez Núñez chose to use the word to title his collection. To opt for such multiplicity in English is key.

in clouds no one is a foreigner
tongue latitude
            blood longitude
matter thinks of and contradicts itself

departure is a parting, a farewell. And yet, while verses and entire stanzas break apart enjambed, here is a conscious choice to be in many places at once, to reject "at-homeness,"[2] to move back and forth. It is exile but it is also origin: Cuba and beyond. It is a response to and a reflection on a very specific kind of journey of migration. *departure* is to leave and to stay.

---

1. In 2016, *despegue* won the most coveted award an unpublished book of poetry in Spanish can receive, the Loewe International Poetry Prize. It was first published with Visor Libros in Spain that same year.

2. Pierre Joris's term in *A Nomadic Poetics* (Wesleyan University Press, 2003) p.26.

country resolute in triangular ruins
breathless on the stairs
no longer here or returning with you

departure is deviating from the expected and the accepted. The poems here are sonnets but intentionally unrhymed, all upper-case letters and punctuation suppressed, the essential orality of poetry underscored. At the same time, they redefine conventional ideas of Cuba. In these pages the reader will not find maracas, cigars, rum, salsa dancing, bearded rebels in army fatigues, picturesque poverty, leftover socialist nostalgia, tropical temptation. *departure* is decidedly not the Cuba demanded.

i have been waiting for you
an eternity
       here and everywhere
at this moment and never

Ultimately, *departure* is innovating. Rodríguez Núñez's poetry is often characterized as hermetic, irrational. On the contrary, it serves as a call to dialogue, as a search for an active reader to aid in the creation of meaning. In so doing, it signals a new path for contemporary Latin American poetry. As translator, I enter the conversation and further it. We await you then, reader, here and everywhere.

Katherine M. Hedeen
Mount Vernon, Ohio
February 2024

i.
salida

i.
exit

MAZORRA

en el pabellón rojo los enfermos
pendientes de la voz como una espada
deletrean la palabra astrolabio
la nada no interrumpe

su discurso borbota de las tumbas
orejas de la muerte
a la sombra rebelde de una ceiba
su voluntad hidráulica

el agua no sigue un solo camino
el sol sabe que se marchitará
por eso en la miseria resplandece

una fuerza verde impulsa la elipsis
la muerte es muda
                    el crisantemo habla por ti

MAZORRA

in the red wing the unwell
awaiting the voice like a sword
spell out the word astrolabe
nothingness does not disturb

its discourse bubbles up from the graves
death ears
in the rebellious shade of a ceiba
its hydraulic will

water does not follow just one path
sun knows it will wither
and so in misery it shines

a green force propels the ellipsis
death is mute
                chrysanthemum speaks for you

SANTA MARÍA

sin media luz donde caerse muerto
tirado en esta playa
como el cangrejo que no tuvo suerte
y el niño perdonó

compadeces a la piedra que te guiña un ojo
su fresca militancia
y la bicicleta cargada de caracoles
te cruza entre las muelas

la arena en las cesuras
hace que las claves no estén en tiempo
el mundo es una güira pintada como quiera

para la discreción de los turistas
nadie te contó antes
lo que se aprende si sales del agua

SANTA MARÍA

no halflight to drop dead under
sprawled on this beach
like the crab luckless
and forgiven by the child

you feel for the stone that winks at you
its fresh militancy
and the bicycle chock full of seashells
crosses you between claws

sand in caesuras
puts claves offbeat
the world is a güiro painted any which way

at the discretion of the tourists
nobody told you before
what you learn if you leave the water

PARQUE CENTRAL

revuelo de palomas
                          el viejo sin camisa
de ánima presente gesticula
la terca luz que sostiene las ruinas

sin duda estorba al cielo
en la ciudad sitiada
                          moscas libres
se cumplen dominós se juegan planes

cuerpos que no trabaja la riqueza
la sangre gris del arroz con frijoles
algo nunca pasó como debía

el carro silba los borrachos frenan
el que fuera un gallardo miliciano
muere por vender fósforos

PARQUE CENTRAL

dove disturbance
                    old man shirtless
with his anima open-casket gesturing
stubborn light holding up the ruins

no doubt obstructing sky
in the city besieged
                    flies free
dominoes kept plans played

bodies not worked by wealth
gray blood of rice and beans
something never happened like it ought to

the car honks the drunks brake
the man once a gallant soldier
dies from selling matches

PLAZA DE LA REVOLUCIÓN

y se apiñan el que da cincel a la mañana
la que carga una puerta
                              por donde no va a entrar
el que deja caer su arroz con leche en la esquina

la sorda de cañón que marca el paso
en ruedas de casino
el que nunca se sienta
                              en sillones de mimbre

la que encuentra un paisaje
al abrir la última lata de vita nova
el que niega el saludo

pero va a la reunión del comité
la que vomita el alma
                              el que vuela esta noche

PLAZA DE LA REVOLUCIÓN

and they gather one chisels the dawn
one carries a door
                         she won't go through
one lets his rice pudding fall at the corner

one deaf as a post keeps the beat
in conga lines
one never sits
                    on wicker rocking chairs

one finds a landscape
when she opens the last can of vita nova
one refuses to say hello

but off to the committee meeting he goes
one vomits up her soul
                        one flies tonight

LA MODERNA POESÍA

nadie dijo que la cosa era así
testarudo diamante
                              y el sistema poético
romper honra con bueyes

cargar el llanto a cubos
                              alma que no descarga
la comparsa resiste
el relumbre sin uso de valor

una calle bajo el cisco de agosto
trincheras de ideas llueven esquirlas
columnas desmochadas

se puede ver el hueso
la poética del subdesarrollo
el cartabón oval

LA MODERNA POESÍA

nobody ever said things were going to be like this
stubborn diamond
                       and the poetic system
to plough honor with oxen

to carry the crying in buckets
                                    soul won't flush
carnival troupe defies
brilliance with no value use

a street beneath august's coaldust
trenches of ideas raining splinters
columns clipped

you can see clear to the bone
the poetics of underdevelopment
the quadrant oval

MALECÓN

el ruso con arpón y la santera
pisan fuerte sobre la savia de flamboyán
no hay sentido común
                              solo hollar la belleza

él ensartará su cubera de oro
coleando en el agua enjabonada
ella se casará con su turista
encantado con la asimetría de los pechos

todo en la misma tarde
en que el sol decidió quedarse fijo
sin embargo la lluvia se apersona

se filtra entre las ruinas
cuando la noche vuelva encontrará
desilusión en sal

MALECÓN

the ruso with his harpoon and the santera
trample the flamboyant treepitch
there is no common sense
                              only treading on beauty

he will string his golden cubera snapper
wagging its tail in the soapy water
she will marry her tourist
bewitched by the asymmetry of her breasts

all of it on the same evening
when the sun decided to stay still
even so the rain appears in person

leaks among the ruins
when night returns it will find
disillusion in salt

CALLE TROCADERO

el despacho de ron una monja por línea
donde el flaco ovaciona
nalgas prietas en uniforme albino
y su potencia médica

deforestada selva de cemento
se tejen celulares
y se recargan alpargatas nórdicas
se sabe el capitalismo funciona

de una oscura manera
se sabe el socialismo no funciona
de una clara manera

un ruido de tres pares de cojones
el avión que fumiga
                       eriza la ciudad

CALLE TROCADERO

the rum stand three pesos a shot
where the skinny man applauds
black backside in albino uniform
and its medical superpower

deforested concrete jungle
cell phones woven here
nordic espadrilles refilled here
everybody knows capitalism works

darkly
everybody knows socialism doesn't work
clearly

so much fucking noise
fumigating plane
                    makes the city bristle

HOTEL TELÉGRAFO

entre las ruinas del hotel telégrafo
que siguen siendo irreales
como carta de amor por internet
y una cerveza cuesta

un ojo de otra cara
el travesti lucha con el teléfono
necesita llamar al paraíso
como el totí prendido del alambre

donde también se orea el firmamento
mientras el temba no le dice nada
se frota los juanetes el prepucio

paga por el silencio y la propina
como *granma* no miente
pero tampoco dice la verdad

HOTEL TELÉGRAFO

in the ruins of the hotel telégrafo
which are still fake
like a loveletter sent online
and a beer costs

someone else's arm and leg
the transvestite locks horns with the telephone
needs to call paradise
like the grackle fastened to the wire

where the firmament too hangs out to dry
while the silver fox doesn't say a thing
just rubs his bunions his foreskin

he pays for the silence and the tip
like *granma* doesn't lie
but doesn't tell the truth either

19 DE MAYO Y AYESTARÁN

se va otro carpintero
a reparar los fustes
                              podridos a porfía
en las granjas estatales del cielo

la clandestina lucha
la cola para el palacio de los matrimonios
el hervor del boniato
los hijos que agarraron comején

fajada la cintura con tres hernias
el pelo racionado irracional
y la zurda sin manga vena a pulso

se va otro carpintero
no solo la madera
                              también los clavos lloran

19 DE MAYO Y AYESTERÁN

another carpenter has gone
to fix the determinedly rotten
                                        shafts
in the state-run farms of heaven

the clandestine struggle
the line for the wedding palace
the boniato boiling
the kids who caught termites

girdled the waist with three hernias
rationed irrational hair
and the sleeveless southpaw freehand vein

another carpenter has gone
it's not just the wood
                        the nails are crying too

CALLE ÁGUILA

el socialismo es una larga espera
como ese ciego que marca y se va
a echarse un cafecito con la suerte
cualquier cosa menos capitalismo

el sol tiene pegada y llueven oros
pero solo la náusea brilla en el asfalto
el almendrón fumiga
y se dispersa este falso cometa

¿en torno a qué se gira?
el perro trasero que olfatea al delantero
se mea contra el carro de valores

el viejo con *juventud rebelde* en el bolsillo
y el sordo que no deja de pedir
                              por el último

CALLE ÁGUILA

socialism is a long wait
like the blind man who calls last in line and goes off
to have a cafecito if he's lucky
anything but capitalism

the sun packs a punch and it's raining golds
but only nausea shines on the asphalt
the almendrón fumigates
and this fake comet scatters

what is it spinning around?
the back dog sniffs the front one
pisses on the armored car

the old man with *juventud rebelde* in his pocket
and the deaf man who won't stop asking

                                    who is last in line

COJÍMAR

el cielo a despejar y la mañana rompe
en los bancos de arena
de la inercia escapas
                    das la espalda a las olas

caminas por la orilla que se hiere
con su filo espumoso
doscientos metros cuadrados de sol
azul en cada esquina

la niña que reúne caracoles
se asusta con la marea encarnada
la orientación política del viento

llueve sobre las balsas golondrinas
sagrada intrascendencia
                    ardua pesca de altura

COJÍMAR

the sky about to clear and the morning breaks
in the sand banks
you escape from the inertia

                              turn your back on the waves

walk along the shore wounded
by its own foamy edge
two hundred square meters of sun
blue at each corner

the little girl who gathers seashells
is frightened by the incarnadine tide
the wind's political position

it rains on balsas swallows
sacred non-transcendence

                         arduous deepsea fishing

CALLE VIRTUDES

eres el panadero
madrugado para amasar la sombra
y sacar una miga a cada libra
la rubia que baldea

                              aunque nada se limpie
y el tiempo se alborote
el palestino entre las amapolas
que ya no sabe qué hacer con la espera

y la buena noticia
                      recibida jamás
avanzas por el fondo irregular

cruzas surcos salidos de los cuartos
y te estremeces solo con la luz
su firmeza ideológica

CALLE VIRTUDES

you are the baker
up early to kneed the shadow
and pull a crumb from each pound
the blonde hoses things down

                         though nothing gets clean
and time gets anxious
the palestino in the poppies
who doesn't know what to do with the wait

and the good news
                never gotten
you move through the uneven background

cross furrows jutting out of rooms
and only shudder with the light
its ideological strength

LA RAMPA

te fuiste por tu cuenta

                         nadie te perseguía

no te faltaban oportunidades

solo querías conocer el mundo

con su unanimidad el verde te irritaba

y buscabas sosiego entre la nieve

¿te fuiste por tu cuenta?

                         ¿nadie te perseguía?

¿no te faltaban oportunidades?

¿solo querías conocer el mundo?

¿con su unanimidad el verde te irritaba?

¿y buscabas sosiego entre la nieve?

entonces ¿qué pasó?

                         ¿y estos calambres rojos?

LA RAMPA

you left on your own
                     nobody came after you
you had plenty of opportunities
just wanted to know the world

with its unanimity the green got under your skin
and you searched for calm in the snow
you left on your own?
                     nobody came after you?

you had plenty of opportunities?
just wanted to know the world?
with its unanimity the green got under your skin?

and you searched for calm in the snow?
so then what happened?
                     why these red crampings?

CEMENTERIO DE ESPADA

fueron hechas las sagradas visitas
en los muros sin hiedra
                           curados por la luz
algo de ti responde

al viento en la cal viva
                           no morirás contigo
cuando no estés todo va a ser igual
uno se queda en otro

solo debes el turno la libreta
hay una sola muerte
                           y la llevas en ti

nunca se deja en casa
                           ni espera en otra esquina
siempre es aquí y ahora

CEMENTERIO DE ESPADA

the sacred visits were made
on the ivyless walls
                          cured by light
something of yours replies

to the wind in the living lime
                              you won't die with you
when you aren't here everything will stay the same
one stays in the other

the appointment the ration book are the only things you owe
there's only one death
                          and you carry it inside you

it is never left at home
                          never waits on another street corner
it is always here and now

RANCHO BOYEROS

uno no viene de ninguna parte
uno no se va nunca
aquí te tienen sudado y ansioso
en la acera del sol la de los negros

sin vuelta o paraíso
                    sin infierno o partida
ni la imaginación ni la memoria
te cambiarán de banda

siempre has estado allá también aquí
no hay otro lugar que este resplandor
milagro constatarlo

y cuando ya no seas
la misma indignación
                    único compromiso

RANCHO BOYEROS

one does not come from nowhere
one never leaves
here they have you sweaty and anxious
on the burning black sidewalk

no return or paradise
                              no hell or parting
no imagination or memory
they will change whose side you're on

you have always been there here too
no other place but this brightness
a miracle to confirm it

and when you are no longer
the same indignation
                              lone commitment

ii.
vuelo

ii.
flight

1

un vuelo sin destino sin origen
como bala de plata
                    en la boca del lobo
la nostalgia agrumada nubarrón

claridad turbulenta
abordo del vacío
                    en su piel de majá
una pluma en la elipse de la noche

la violencia cubierta
                    con maleza celeste
fijeza inalcanzable trayectoria

como rayo de albur
                    adentrarse en el día
en el destierro también amanece

1

a flight no destination no origin
like a silver bullet
                    in the wolf's mouth
nostalgia curdled stormcloud

clarity turbulent
aboard the void
                    in its majá skin
a feather in the night ellipse

violence shrouded
                    in celestial underbrush
fixedness unreachable trajectory

like a bolt of fate
                    to go deep into the day
in exile it also dawns

2

entre las nubes nadie es extranjero
latitud de la lengua
                              longitud de la sangre
materia que se piensa y contradice

agua vapor escarcha
rápido de los andes témpano de noruega
lágrima de caimán
                              transpiración

nunca tropiezas con la misma gota
con el otro carámbano
sino la turbulencia que entrecruza las penas

su comercio intangible
                              estela de lo informe
eres el compatriota de las nubes

2

in clouds no one is a foreigner
tongue latitude
                    blood longitude
matter thinks of and contradicts itself

water steam frost
andes rapid norway ice floe
caiman tear
              perspiration

you never run into the same drop
into the other icicle
instead the turbulence that intertwines sorrows

its intangible commerce
                            wake of what is shapeless
you are the compatriot of clouds

3

a golpe de guitarra se alza vuelo
paloma impopular
doble capa de cúmulos
y el índigo imperioso

surca un barco el abismo
seguido por la conga y el naufragio
la linda americana no acompaña
su sinuoso compás

como todo verano en alas de la madre
se entona un son estático
las claves y su de dónde serás

el espacio responde sin fe sin ilusión
trova relampagueante
el corazón como trompeta china

3

to take flight by force of thrum
unpopular dove
twin layers of cumulus
and imperious indigo

a ship plows through the abyss
followed by conga and shipwreck
the pretty american doesn't play along
her sinuous rhythm

like each summer on mother wings
a static rumba intones
the claves and their i wonder where you're froms

space answers back no faith no illusion
trova flashing
heart like a trompeta china

4

colgado a la razón
                    que acalambra la nube
la oración a san lázaro
rigurosa como la aerodinámica

la atómica central
                    sitiada por el bosque
el río atravesado
por la ciudad para drenar el sueño

al canto del celaje
                    la belleza descalza
dejándose leer sin moraleja

como paisaje de otro
esa oración donde ondulas
                    y te ases

4

hung on the reason
                              that cramps the cloud
the prayer to san lázaro
exact like aerodynamics

the nuclear powerplant
                              besieged by the forest
the river crossed
by the city to drain the dream

on the edge of the cloudscape
                              beauty barefoot
letting herself be read there is no moral

like another's landscape
the prayer where you sway
                              and hold on

5

en el cielo de nadie
médula del estar una parábola
es tu sombra y su nube
sobre el fondo esmaltado chinería

el golfo la península
se dejan enmarcar por el grafito
sobre papel de arroz
el barco enajenado

                        se deshace del humo
volar no te hace libre
el destino queda en manos del viento

un azul sin riberas con sentido
te quemará las manos
limbo de todas partes que se invierte

5

in nobody's sky
the staying's marrow a parabola
it is your shadow and its cloud
on the enameled background chinoiserie

the gulf the peninsula
let themselves be framed by the graphite
on rice paper
the ship deranged

                              gets rids of the smoke
flying does not make you free
destiny is in the hands of the wind

a blue shoreless not senseless
will burn your hands
limbo from everywhere inside out

6

con el sol a la izquierda
vuelas de un hijo a otro
                              triangulado
en el vacío del pecho

el azul es el susto
                         que se lleva la altura
el cirro a palo seco
música anaranjada

la mañana es un salto de venado
y nieve refundida
a la sombra de un cuervo

entraña transparente
¿se merecen los hijos en sus vórtices
que te cortes las alas?

6

with the sun on the left
you fly from one child to another
                              triangulated
in the chest vacuum

blue is what
                gives height a scare
the cirrus straight up
orange music

the morning is a deerleap
and snow meltdown
in the shadow of a crow

transparent insides
do your children in their vortexes deserve
for you to clip your wings?

7

otra vez avispado pero en el horizonte
en alas no de la imaginación
del sentido común
                    y su acerado viento

unas alas en cruz
                    con nostalgia de clavos
abuso de razón
                    la memoria al revés

sin la gravitación de la casida
que te empina sobre el diente de perro
extático en la nube

                    espasmo de azafata
entre el presente y tú como el insomnio
un destino emplumado

7

once more skittish but on the horizon
on the wings not of imagination
of common sense
                        and its steely wind

wings crossed
                    with a nostalgia for nails
abuse of reason
                        memory backwards

no qasida gravitation
to raise you above the dogtooth
ecstatic on the cloud

                        stewardess spasm
between the present and you like the insomniac
a feathered destiny

8

en el viento hay sales que germinan
de súbito sin ninguna intención
el sentimiento helado
                    se despega de sí

se enraíza invisible
es cantil increpado por la escarcha
con su seca belleza
                    y su húmeda verdad

mas se huele la duda
del que ganó la piel en el combate
y regresa a su otra casa de arena

este soplo que se llena de pámpanos
la materia de toda reflexión
dios es impresionista

8

in the wind there are salts sprouting
suddenly without any intention
the frozen sentiment
                              comes apart

takes root unseen
is cliff rebuked by the frost
with its dry beauty
                              and wet truth

but you can smell the doubt
of the one who earned his skin in combat
and returns to his other house of sand

this gust filling with vine shoots
the matter of every reflection
god is impressionistic

9

se desgarra la nube y aparece
una tierra arrugada
                    un cuerno de elefante
un aire que solo traslada vértigo

la nube es una artesa de sentido
absorbe el significado que le pertenece
y sin embargo ondea
                    puede tomar altura

la nube rastrillada sin plantar
que ha visto demasiado
                    y se adensa con ira

la nube mal pintada sobre una sierra ajena
solo quiere ser lluvia
                    y dejarse caer

9

torn open the cloud and a wrinkled
land emerges
                    an elephant horn
a wind that only transfers vertigo

the cloud is a sense trough
it absorbs the meaning that belongs to it
and still it ripples
                    can take on height

the cloud raked unplanted
has seen too much
                    and grows thick with ire

the cloud badly painted above another's sierra
only wants to be rain
                    and to let itself fall

10

no basta con la huella
                         se precisa el error
bracear fuera de cámara
no esperes que el miedo te dé una mano

requeridos la altura
                         remontar turbulencias
no creer más en ti estar atento
cada instante toda una noche en claro

hincar una familia vertical
al encanto del sitio
esto como el amor no se hace solo

aunque el después se ausente como el antes
eres raíz con miedo
                         deseo y algo más

10

not enough the trace
                        error pinpointed
to paddle away from the camera
don't wait for fear to lend you a hand

required the altitude
                        to soar above turbulences
to stop believing in you to be alert
every instant an entire night white

to drive a vertical family
into the charm of the place
this like love is not made alone

though the after is gone like the before
you are fearful root
                        desire and something more

11

de los huesos se levanta la luna
níquel efervescente
y entre campos de nubes en secano
alguien vuelve a cantar

pero la r de piaf
                    no es miel en el café
la visión se da vuelta
no se arrepentirá de ser la sal

con rabia de partir a corazón abierto
calado en savia roja
                    la conjura

despegue horizontal
flecha adversa
                    no darás en el blanco

11

from the bones rises the moon
effervescent nickel
and among cloudfields in dry land
someone sings again

but piaf's r
                    is not sweetness in the coffee
the vision goes round
won't regret being salt

with the rage of parting openheart
soaked in red sap
                    the plot

horizontal departure
adverse arrow
                    you won't hit the bullseye

12

como el agua en la arena
                        buscas una salida
ya no puedes ser estrato ni escarcha
porque pesan las ganas

un pasajero más desorientado
lees en la pizarra tu destino
este viaje en redondo
                        y a deshora

ya no hay nadie a tu lado
                        salvo la lejanía
en una ardiente víspera

donde se tejen tarrayas sin puntos
un río que refluye
                        el mar no es la salida

12

like water in sand
                       you search for an exit
now you cannot be stratum or frost
because the want weighs on you

one more passenger mislead
you read your destiny on the monitors
this trip a round
                       and at the wrong time

now there's nobody beside you
                              except the far off
in a burning eve

where nets are woven unstitched
a river surging
                   the sea is not the exit

13

en las nubes la vida

                    te grava como nunca

otro modo impensable del estar

ampararse en el aire

                  la finta de ascender

al menos aspirar esta fatiga

triángulos desteñidos

ojales sin red que se superponen

¿el sentido del viaje?

                      ¿un pueblo empantanado?

¿la almendrilla de cielo en la rodilla?

mas la vida te exime en el descenso

cuando la aeromoza pliega tu mesa

y te apoyas en nada la zozobra

13

in the clouds life
                        crushes you like never before
another unthinkable way of staying
safeguard in the air

                        the feint of ascending
at least inhaling this fatigue
triangles faded
redless eyelets overlapping

the sense of the journey?
                              a people bogged down?
the sky shavings under your knee?

but life frees you on the descent
when the stewardess closes your tray table
and you hold on to nothing the fall

14

la cicatriz de un río
                        cruza el rostro de nadie
como el abeto interrumpe la nieve
sin dar explicaciones

nacen vientos cruzados
y desordenan la imaginación
recuas de nubes grises
y entre ellas una preñada de luz

volar entre dos vidas
que la luna creciente no puede revelar
con su anillo escarchado

desde el puente rasguea
                        ideogramas la sangre
en algún lugar debe estar el sol

14

the scar of a river
                              crosses nobody's face
like the fir tree disrupts the snow
with no explanation

crosswinds are born
and clutter the imagination
packs of gray clouds
and among them one pregnant with light

to fly between two lives
unrevealed by the crescent moon
with its frosty ring

from the bridge blood
                              strokes ideograms
the sun must be somewhere

15

aún entre las nubes
sin espacio para una gleba más
esta tarde encarnada desorillas
espigadas razones

una nueva oración
no vas a ser la lluvia deseada
por el aroma del campo de col
y el que solo procura estar desnudo

a golpe de soneto terminal
el lago se coagula en la sombra
pero la serranía se rebela

y el crepúsculo crece alas en todo
muñón desenraizado
las nubes son una forma de melancolía

15

still in the clouds
no room for one more clod
this evening flesh-colored you edgeweed
sprigged reasons

a new prayer
you won't be the rain desired
by the aroma of the cabbage patch
and the one who only wants to get undressed

by the force of a terminal sonnet
the lake clots in the shade
but the mountains rebel

and twilight grows wings in it all
uprooted stump
the clouds are a kind of melancholy

iii.
escala

iii.
stopover

OHIO RIVER VALLEY

ya viene el horizonte
puedo escuchar su luz
                que tropieza con todo
y me deja la piel con sabor a jengibre

ya se deja empuñar
la z materna del río ohio
sus fábricas de noche electoral
sus almacenes de desasosiego

ya las casas en mí
como remaches sobre el fuselaje
de un avión en el iris de un tornado

y el descenso hacia ti
                sonrisa izquierda
y el abrigo que me empieza a extrañar

OHIO RIVER VALLEY

now comes the horizon
i can hear its light
                        trip on everything
it leaves my skin with a taste of ginger

now letting itself be gripped
the ohio river's maternal z
its election night factories
its anxiety warehouses

now the homes in me
like rivets on the fuselage
of a plane in the iris of a tornado

and the descent toward you
                        leftist smile
and the winter coat beginning to miss me

WILLAMETTE VALLEY

el sol ebanista bruñe el estanque
mas el viento no está para resinas
la cuestión es la vaca
con ubres como un huevo

enraizado en el hambre
la cabeza volada de su sombra
se posa en un ciprés
emocionado por algún deceso

entre todas las formas
se entromete la noche desvelada
una cópula entre cepillo y ola

el viento atiza con olor a pino
en el centro lo que nunca se cuenta
la mancha resentida

WILLAMETTE VALLEY

woodworker sun burnishes the pond
but the wind is not up for resins
the issue is the cow
with udders like an egg

deeprooted in hunger
head flying away from its shadow
perches on a cypress
excited for some death date

among all the shapes
sleepless night barges in
a copula between brush and wave

wind stirs with a scent of pine
in the middle what is never said
resentful stain

GARY'S SHOP

se apila la madera como sílabas
insomnios de verlaine
y se pone a secar
                    con sed de nieve

abeto roble cedro
el hacha ya editó
                    los nudos suspensivos
solo restan las fibras de calor

¿qué hacer con las babosas
las pausas que gotean
                    y las culebras verdes?

el reuma llega al alma
rendidos los guantes de leñador
arde la misma niebla

GARY'S SHOP

wood piles up like syllables
verlaine's insomnias
it begins to dry out
                    with a snow's thirst

fir oak cedar
the ax already edited
                    the suspension knots
only the heat fibers are left

what to do with the slugs
the pauses dripping
                    and the green snakes?

rheumatism reaches the soul
worn out the woodcutter gloves
burning the very mist

MILK CREEK

único ser alerta en la familia
a esta hora inocente
en la distancia pulsan los disparos
ebrios sin ilusión

                    de la basura blanca
en la proximidad el fuego ronca
un poco incómodo en la nueva estufa
regalo de enemigo

la noche se prepara a recibir
en un porrazo de agua
                    el año fermentado

y después a dormir sin previsiones
entre sábanas bruscas
no habrá sueño que ladre

MILK CREEK

lone attentive being in the family
at this innocent hour
far off drunken with no illusions
the gunshots

               of the white trash pulsate
close by the fire snoring
a little uneasy in the new stove
gift from the enemy

night gets ready to receive
with a toss of water
                   the fermented year

and later to sleep with no previsions
on rough sheets
no dream barking

POWELL'S BOOKS

esa flor con historia
no hará oler mejor esta casida
la piedra soñada por el joyero
no la iluminará

está escrito en la corteza de un árbol
extraviado en el bosque
¿restar casualidades
                    adicionar esencias?

no hay fórmula para esta levadura
todo se forma a pulso
                    ojo de buen cubero

la inspiración es un cero a la izquierda
está escrito en el moho
                    no en la roca

POWELL'S BOOKS

flower with history
won't make this qasida smell any better
the stone dreamed by the jeweler
won't brighten it

it is written on the bark of a tree
gone missing in the forest
to minus chances?
                        to add essences?

no formula for this yeast
everything takes shape freehand
                                eyeballing

inspiration is a zero to the left
it is written in the mold
                        not in the rock

EDGEFIELD

tsagaglalal espía
y sus pupilas huelen a jazmín
¿qué vas a hacer con toda esa virtud
que te curte las manos?

algo bueno hicimos porque nos mira
con fijeza como a los valles rojos
ese instante en que calla la montaña
y se pueden decir algunas cosas

entre los dos volcanes apagados una c
el río en retirada del desierto
su jadeo también huele a guayaba

te descobijo desde que coyote
arribó a nixluidix
nada es para siempre salvo el amor

EDGEFIELD

tsagaglalal keeps watch
and her pupils smell like jasmine
what are you going to do with all that virtue
weathering your hands?

we did something good because she stares
at us like the red valleys
the moment when the mountains quiets
and you can say some things

between two dormant volcanos a c
the river in retreat from the desert
its panting smells like guava too

i have uncovered you since coyote
arrived in nixluidix
nothing is forever except love

HAWTHORNE LANE

la perra que hace un verano ladraba
a su sombra gatuna
si en un descuido la dejaba sola
y trepaba al cogollo de la pícea

llaga en el suelo de madera doble
mientras el viento le alborota el pelo
cuando se abre la puerta
y una sombra erizada

la memoria de su ferocidad
hace volverse loco por espinas
al bigote estañado

todos evitan sin razón pisarla
con la huella celeste
un domingo de oraciones perdidas

HAWTHORNE LANE

the dog who last summer barked
at her feline shadow
if you accidently left her alone
and would climb up to the top of the spruce

with sores on the double wood floor
while the wind stirs up her hair
when the door opens
a bristling shadow

the remembrance of her ferocity
makes her tinplated whiskers
go crazy for fishbones

for no reason everyone avoids stepping on her
with celestial footprints
a sunday of lost prayers

HELEN'S SEWING ROOM

la casa bendecida por la seda
en bastidor de mimbre
oraciones en cinta
                    atemperan el norte

flores estampadas en la pared
para almizclar el sueño
patrones y medidas
                    descarte del error

se cala en el tejido
al pie de un arcoíris de tijeras
ninguna puerta atranca

                    entornada vigilia
todo en un meticuloso desorden
el mundo por zurcir

HELEN'S SEWING ROOM

the house blessed by silk
in a wicker taboret
prayers in ribbon
                    calm the north

flowers stamped on the wall
to perfume sleep with musk
patterns and measures
                    error discarded

broderie anglaise in the fabric
at the foot of a scissor rainbow
no door closes

                vigil ajar
everything a meticulous mess
the world to mend

MOLALLA

en la logia del arce capítulo molalla
bajo barba y peluca se pelean
el rumbero y la rubia de platino
luego se baila ron se fuma mambo

se beben largos tabacos torcidos
se silba con acento
                              todo de utilería
para felicidad de la basura blanca

nadie se asusta aquí
                              si la vida da un vuelco
el futuro es pasado no previsto

y el presente no se puede pagar
con tarjeta de crédito
entre todos se entona babalú

MOLALLA

in the moose lodge molalla chapter
beneath beard and wig argue
the rumbero and the platinum blonde
afterwards rum is danced and mambo smoked

long twisted cigars drunk
whistle with an accent
                              everything is props
to the delight of the white trash

nobody is scared here
                              if life turns upside down
the future is the unexpected past

and the present cannot be paid
with a credit card
all together they croon babalú

27 MALLARD POINTE

de súbito en tu casa
                         que ya no reconoces
ni te reconoce peor aún
aunque has dejado fibras de adn

en todas sus aristas
y has cargado contigo varios cielos
algún fondo de mar
ya ves no te será dado volver

a orillas de este lago imaginado
se olvidará tu lengua
se dirán cosas con letras inútiles

no te quites esa sombra arrugada
ni la mirada zurda
aquí también eres un extranjero

27 MALLARD POINTE

suddenly at the home
                              you no longer recognize
and worse still doesn't recognize you
though you have left dna fibers

on all its edges
you have lugged it with you various skies
some sea bottoms
now you know it won't return to you

at the shores of this imagined lake
your language will be forgotten
things with useless letters uttered

don't shake off that wrinkled shadow
or the leftist gaze
here you are a stranger too

MOUNT HOOD

la cama donde fuiste concebida
a espaldas del invierno puritano
en la noche se tuerce
                    al peso del estar

una araña en la altura
su sentido traspuesto al rojo vivo
en busca de un pezón
                    donde ocultarse

llegaste en la ceniza
casi se estrella el alma contra el vértice
nevado con rigor

herido en su avidez
                    como un viento sin pájaros
el sol sale mañana entre tus pechos

MOUNT HOOD

the bed where you were conceived
behind the back of the puritan winter
buckles in the night
                    under the weight of the staying

a spider on high
its sense transplanted red hot
in search of a nipple
                    to hide in

you came here in ash
soul almost slamming against vertex
snowed on rigorously

wounded in its desire
                    like a birdless wind
the sun will rise tomorrow from your breasts

OREGON CITY

entre un azulejo que salta desde la hierba
con la primera luz
                              y un verso de szymborska
contra los desencuentros de la muerte

te quedas con la duda
                              su tallo inoxidable
su corola geométrica
espigan los escombros

                              a manos del rocío
su terca sed celeste
                    la rima de otro mundo

significante sin significado
cada cosa una voz
                    con nada que decir

OREGON CITY

between a bluebird hopping from the grass
with the first light
                    and a verse by szymborksa
against the mixups of death

you have a lingering doubt
                        its rustproof stem
its geometric corolla
the rubble runs to seed

                    at the hands of the dew
its stubborn celestial thirst
                    another world rhyme

non-signified signifier
every thing a voice
                with nothing to say

MANZANITA

paralelo al deseo
que se aviva con la marea baja
entre huesos de mar
                        contra un aire sin huellas

la luz acomete por todas partes
pájaro carpintero
                        su trova medieval
la sustancia nocturna del pacífico

se concentra en la copa veneciana
donde solo el crepúsculo ha probado
su favila de niebla

con precisión todo allí se abandona
y no vaya a pasar
este instante que da para una vida

MANZANITA

parallel to desire
rekindled by low tide
in seabones
                against a traceless wind

the light attacks from all sides
woodpecker
                its medieval ballad
the nocturnal substance of the pacific

it pools in the venetian glass
where only twilight has tried
its hazy ember

with precision everything there is abandoned
don't let it get away
this instant enough to last a lifetime

PORT COLUMBUS

hace una eternidad
que te espero
                    aquí y en todas partes
en este instante y nunca

yo no puedo acudir donde tú esperas
he perdido el compás
soy norte impreciso
                    reloj de luna

como el avión inmóvil
en el añil con otra dirección
vadeo las tormentas los tormentos

en el punto de origen y final
pese a la renuncia a la puntuación
juego este solitario consonante

PORT COLUMBUS

i have been waiting for you
an eternity
                    here and everywhere
at this moment and never

i cannot get to where you are waiting
i have lost the compass
i am imprecise north
                              moon dial

like the unmoving plane
in the indigo with another destination
i ford the tempests the torments

at the point of origin and end
despite giving up the punctuation
i play this consonant solitaire

NEAH-KAH-NIE

y la luz se derroca
desde el cometa surgido del mar
como un hilo de agua entre las fieras
que la sed petrifica

los cangrejos de alaska
                         erratas del estar
se internan en el bosque
bordadas en el viento las gaviotas

descreídas de sí
toda memoria pronto será fango
dorado por el liquen

delicias sin jardín
                        alarmas de tsunami
desde la espuma gritas

NEAH-KAH-NIE

and the light is defrocked
from the comet looming up from the sea
like a thread of water among the beasts
petrified by thirst

alaskan crabs
                    the staying's typos
go deeper into the forest
embroidered in the wind the seagulls

unbelievers of themselves
every memory suddenly mud
gilded by the lichen

delights gardenless
                        tsunami warnings
from the foam you cry out

iv.
puerto

iv.
port

1

un corazón discorde
no crees en el sistema donde tienes hogar
nunca te dio un hogar el sistema en que crees
arreas tu ganado tropical

por un maizal helado
y reclinas la cabeza traslúcida
ante los vapores de un majarete
nadie te echó nadie te pidió que te quedaras

cuando te fuiste cuando regresaste
no cayeron en cuenta
todos más desahogados que después

no lates por nostalgia
sino porque el ingenio demolido
acaba de silbar no sé qué hora

1

a heart out of tune
you do not believe in the system where you have a home
the system you believe in never gave you one
you rustle your tropical cattle

through a frozen cornfield
lean back your translucent head
before the steaming dish of majarete
nobody kicked you out nobody asked you to stay

when you left when you came back
they did not notice
everyone less crowded than after

you do not beat from nostalgia
but from the torn down sugar mill
just now whistling i don't know what shift

2

despiertas entre pájaros y no das el si
un petirrojo en su circunferencia
contra el jazmín de noche
bajo el sueño las alas no dejan de batir

entre el abismo y tú
                         este fino metal
una aleación soñada
su resplandor poderoso e ingrávido

el baño en la ceniza te libra de la sed
un sueño como azófar
tus raíces no lo pueden cuartear

eres lo que se esconde
en la misma rama donde el halcón
desplumó otro revuelo

2

you wake up in birds and you don't reach the b
a robin in its circumference
against the night jasmine
beneath the dream its wings don't stop flapping

between the abyss and you
                              this fine metal
a dreamt-of alloy
its brilliance powerful weightless

bathing in ash frees you from thirst
a dream like brass
your roots can't quarter it

you are what is hidden
in the same branch where the hawk
fleeced another fluttering

3

en esta encrucijada
                    bajo otra tempestad
el gallo muerto por las muy piadosas
manos del babalao

un sentimiento sube
                    por la húmeda escala
hasta donde no irradia la ceguera
a coro tres testigos

elevan la canción sin desplumar
saciada por la sed a cántaros caída
lleva corona recia el babalao

cortada del crepúsculo
y un cuerpo imperceptible
                    que la lluvia no toca

3

at this crossroads
                     beneath another storm
the rooster killed by the oh so pious
hands of the babalao

a sentiment rises up
                     through the damp stairstep
to where blindness does not radiate
in unison three witnesses

raise the song without fleecing
it is satiated by the thirst fallen in torrents
the babalao wears a fierce crown

cut from twilight
and an imperceptible body
                     untouched by the rain

4

primer rayo de sol
                    sin clara consecuencia
detrás de la cortina con flores de otra edad
sillas apuñaleadas

la v donde debes alzar la voz
esta revelación canto de gallo
silba la cafetera en tu lugar
al olfatear la noche

también jadea el polvo intransigente
con su lámpara ciega
interesada como todo amor

hogar es donde estás
en la leche cortada
                    en el pan tomas nota

4

first ray of sun
                  no clear consequence
behind the flower-print curtains from another time
chairs stabbed with a knife

the v where you should raise your voice
this revelation rooster crow
the coffeepot whistles in your place
when it sniffs out night

the diehard dust pants too
with its blind lamp
opportunist like every love

home is where you are
in the curdled milk
                  on the bread you take notes

5

en este patio donde pasa todo
entre arecas zunzunes y malangas
arena de los días no vividos
celeste agricultura

no hay tiempo solo espacio
una luz majadera
renuente a echar raíces como tú
y todo sucede en el mismo instante

una planicie abrupta un astro ya citado
entre ruinas romanas
el maíz constelado de luciérnagas

mordido por la desesperación
ladras con esperanza
en tu médula la lluvia de mayo

5

on this patio where everything happens
amid areca palms hummingbirds and taro plants
sand of days unlived
celestial agriculture

there is no time only space
an unruly light
reluctant to put down roots like you
and everything arises all at once

an abrupt flatland a star already mentioned
amid roman ruins
the corn constellated with fireflies

bitten by desperation
you bark hopeful
the may rains in your marrow

6

cuando apagas la vela
se encienden los sillones de la sala
oscilan como ahorcados
y las chancletas crujen sin pisar

en gallego se insultan entre sí
siguen el ritmo chocando sus huesos
que en la vigilia emergen
de la nieve quemada sin memoria

la sombra quiere aparecer desnuda
vas a cruzar el puente
con un miedo oxidado cardinal

es tiempo de quedarse en todas partes
al menos el ciruelo ha florecido
en el fondo del sueño está la muerte

6

when you blow out the candle
the chairs in the living room switch on
oscillate like hanged men
and the flip-flops creak without taking a step

they call each other names in galician
follow the rhythm hitting their bones
in sleeplessness they surface
from the snow burnt with no memory

the shadow wants to show up naked
you are going to cross the bridge
with a rusty cardinal fear

it is time to stay everywhere
at least the plum tree has blossomed
in the depths of the dream is death

7

severa ley del trópico la mirada oblicua
del sombrero de guano
y la parpadeante estrella de mar
el lenguaje se quita la camisa

se pone a abanicarte
al ritmo del terral las raíces abrazan
almácigo y ateje
su sombra te fulmina como rayo

no te deja soñar despabilarte
la avidez se perfuma
se besa hasta los dientes moretones

la imagen se cuartea por la lluvia
con sus nervios en ascuas
las tormentas salen de los espejos

7

severe law of the tropics the crosswise look
from the palmleaf hat
and the twinkling seastar
language takes off its shirt

it starts fanning you
to the rhythm of the landbreeze the roots embrace
gumbo-limbo and ateje trees
their shade strikes you down like lightning

won't let you dream get your act together
lust wears perfume
kissing even teeth lovebites

image quartered by the rain
with its nerves in embers
torments rise from mirrors

8

con el sol se levantan las preguntas
como ronchas divinas
eres el sábalo que desecha el japonés
mientras caligrafía en el arroz

en voz alta el viento te contradice
se anuda con la luz
el palito izquierdo del japonés
le ha negado al derecho la palabra

si la verdad intenta separarlos
gozan más la rutina su wasabi
eructo de té en la boca del termo

el verano es insomnio con picadas
no te verán la cola la ventrecha
tocas madera pero está podrida

8

with the sun rise questions
like celestial hives
you are the shad the japanese man throws out
while he calligraphs on rice

the wind contradicts you out loud
it is tied to the light
the japanese man's left stick
won't give the floor to the right one

if truth tries to keep them apart
they enjoy the routine their wasabi more
tea belch in the mouth of the thermos

summer is sleepless with bites
the fish belly the fish tail won't see you
you knock on wood but it's rotten

9

una sábana con un agujero
¿qué hacer con lo que falta?
en su centro deben cantar los gallos
nada se despereza

ni la chica ojerosa
descarnada en el sueño por un tigre
se robaron la nieve las urracas
y el paisaje se ha quedado en los huesos

día rebanado en el filo
                              de otro horizonte
noche en que rompe a hervir la manzanilla

con los nudillos cuentas sinalefas
simbólico algodón lavado a mano
donde nada se lee

9

a bedsheet with a hole
what to do with what's missing?
in its middle the roosters ought to crow
nothing stretches out

not even the puffy-eyed girl
flesh torn away by a tiger in a dream
ravens stole the snow
and the landscape lingers in its bones

day slit on the cutting edge
                              of another horizon
night where chamomile comes to a boil

on your knuckles you count synalephas
symbolic cotton washed by hand
where nothing is read

10

la pareja llegó a su palomar
cada uno en su ser en su quehacer
se mueven sin motivo entre los grises
del cielo fracturado

los fregados en seco
                    los cordones de hormiga
los metales que desafió el salitre
la sopa de vapor en espiral

insomnio con estribos
                    reguetón impotente
estas letras sudadas seminales

el último en la mítica azotea
su soledad frugal
                    infiel masturbación

the couple arrived at their dovecote
each in their being in their chores
moving for no reason among the grays
of the fractured sky

the dry dishwashing
                              the rows of ants
metals challenge the saltpeter
soup made of spiraling steam

sleepless with stirrups
                              impotent reggaeton
these letters sweaty seminal

the last one on the mythical rooftop
his frugal solitude
                              unfaithful masturbation

11

es la primera fiebre
de la belleza urdida
                    como plan quinquenal
un primero de mayo

en los altos el perro no deja de ladrar
a la cola del lunes
que fluctúa como mercado negro
una baja silente

en el moskovich del fabulador
ingresa al hospital de parsimonia
virus del paraíso

                    cruzada imperialista
el hambre redundante
y el portero te cede su merienda

11

it is the first fever
of beauty plotted
                    like a five-year plan
a first of may

upstairs the dog won't stop barking
at monday's tail
fluctuating like the black market
a silent casualty

in the fabulist's moskovich
admitted to unurgent care
paradise virus

                    imperialist crusade
surplus hunger
the doorman lets you have his snack

12

un aspa cada mano
los obreros avanzan en su inmovilidad
las latas de pintura sin color
se perlan al rocío

pregona el panadero
y cuando lo buscas se desvanece
el caballo alado caracolea
donde empieza la luz a parpadear

brigadas de gorriones
se disputan tu bilis voluntaria
cuajada en el alfeizar

con los gallos se levanta el vacío
el agua llegó al fin
                    su perreta en el tanque

a blade each hand
the workers advance in their stillness
the cans of colorless paint
pearling with the dew

the baker hawking
but when you go to find him he disappears
the winged horse prances
where the light begins to blink

sparrow brigades
fight over your voluntary bile
curdled on the windowsill

with the roosters rises the void
the water finally came
                       its tantrum in the tank

13

es ola este soneto
que se le vuela al ser en un descuido
y te quema los ojos
                    con su miel negativa

como el caribe brujo la caricia salobre
cuerpo sin redimir recién hurtado
a la corriente
                    al bronco capital

como amor olvidado en la corteza
de una palmera que no crece en público
mas de todas formas echa racimo

y sonoro te mancha
                            iracunda resina
penumbra exponencial

13

it is a wave this sonnet
in an oversight it flies away from being
it burns your eyes
                    with its negative honey

like the bewitching caribbean the salty caress
body unredeemed eaten away
in the current
                    in the rough capital

like love forgotten on the bark
of a palm tree that doesn't grow in public
but sprouts a raceme anyway

resounding it stains you
                        irritable resin
exponential penumbra

14

un sol que raja el ser
                        utópicos mendrugos
se arriman las gaviotas porque sí
pican su saciedad

nada lejos de aquí de la otra orilla
donde comienza todo nuevamente
un punto de descargue
en aguas profundas puerto sin mapa

estar en la memoria desdoblado
terquedad arenosa
fermento de las olas verticales

y al pairo del presente
                        naufragar
un velero encallado en una estrella

14

a sun that slices being open
                              utopic crumbs
the seagulls show up just because
peck at their satiation

nothing far from here from the other side
where everything starts up all over again
discharge point
in deep waters mapless port

to be in memory unfolded
sandy stubbornness
vertical wave ferment

and to heave to in the present
                              to shipwreck
a sailboat run aground on a star

un salto sin vacío
                        al barroco calor
veloz entre la bruma
como un cometa en fuga de su elipse

con el alma y los pies
                            al frío hospitalario
la luz es la respuesta
aunque siempre pregunte en otro idioma

un muro no separa más bien une
con los miedos al aire
                            las arterias en flor

luz que como todo ya no quiere irse
estás del otro lado
                    esperando por mí

a leap voidless
                    into the baroque heat
fast in the seamist
like a comet fleeing its ellipse

with soul and feet
                    in the hospitable cold
light is the answer
even though it always asks in a different language

a wall does not separate it actually unifies
with its fears out in the open
                          its arteries in bloom

light like everything else now doesn't want to leave
you are there on the other side
                          waiting for me

v.
entrada

v.
entrance

CAMPANARIO 158

ante todo raspar
                    todo lo que se ve
la patria está en las claves
el gallo de ciudad que despabila el tráfico

y después dar piqueta
en las partes húmedas alardosas
la patria es tierra firme
sostenida por raíces de mangle

en su sed de color la realidad
absorbe lo que el ciego
le procura con las cerdas de equino

puede ser un islote una mujer
y si aprietas un sueño
es requerida la segunda mano

CAMPANARIO 158

first to scrape away
                        everything you see
the homeland is in the claves
the city rooster waking up traffic

and later to pickaxe
in the damp brazen parts
the homeland is solid ground
held up by mangrove roots

in its thirst for color reality
soaks up what the blind man
gets for it with equine bristles

it can be an islet a woman
and if you pressure a dream
you always need a second coat

AGRO DE ÁNIMAS

el gallo en el mercado de la esquina
saca a puro valor
                al niño bien vestido
que tumba tres macetas de geranios

los borrachos alaban con engolfadas plumas
con pieles de gallina
la carrera a las faldas de la madre
estremecida ante el arrastre de alas

pétalos discursivos contrapuntos
que pueden descrestar
hasta a una polizona del mayflower

el gallo se sacude
             el polvo ineludible
y el premio es una cáscara de plátano

AGRO DE ÁNIMAS

the rooster at the corner market
with pure pluck kicks out
                              the well-dressed child
who's just knocked over three geranium plants

with feathers puffed
with goosebumps the drunks praise
the running back to the apron strings of a mother
shaken before the winged pass made

petals discursive counterpoints
they can impress
even a mayflower stowaway

the rooster shakes off
                              the inevitable dust
the prize is a banana peel

REGLA

un oleaje lustroso
                con arrestos de lámpara
se rompe el espinazo contra el muro
el práctico del puerto

apura su gaseosa de limón
parte hacia el horizonte
un viejo barco acierta la bahía
saluda la bandera

                con bramido oxidado
no se inmuta el jamelgo
metrado por su roja campanilla

los tres turistas lelos en el coche
aguas territoriales
donde el estar sin sombra se va a pique

REGLA

a lustrous stormsurge
                         with lamp darings
breaks its backbone against the wall
the pilot at the dock

gulps down his lemon-lime soda
parts for the horizon
an old ship gets the bay right
greets the flag

                         with a rusty roaring
the nag doesn't bat an eye
metered by its tiny red bell

the three halfwitted tourists in the car
territorial waters
where shadeless staying sinks

VARADERO

trípodes invertidos
                            bajo el viento salobre
donde giran las cobijas de palma
cuerpos que se disputan

                            la penumbra en astillas
alineados al borde
de las olas que dan por donde quiera
y se cubren el rostro precavidos

mientras entregan los pechos al sol
¿quién puede ser feliz con una tos purísima
esa mosca perpetua

                        arena en la mirada?
no obstante el sol se pone
tras la nevada montaña de sillas

VARADERO

upturned tripods
                        beneath the briny wind
where palm canopies spin
bodies disputing

                        the penumbra in splinters
lined up on the edge
of the waves going any which way
covering their faces cautiously

while they hand their breasts over to the sun
who could be happy with a such a pure cough
the perpetual fly

                        sand in the glance?
still the sun sets
behind the snow-capped mountain of chairs

EL ANCÓN

contra toda evidencia los turistas
también tienen una vida que dejar atrás
hay marcas en los cuerpos
del negocio donde afinan sus horas

bajo este sol caníbal
doran sus almas de civilizados
entre los decibeles del oleaje
se asordan sus angustias

pero el terral atiza el sueño de alas
las esencias espuman
y se escurren entre las apariencias

al cabo sobreviven el placer
vuelven a sus asuntos
                    los castillos de arena

EL ANCÓN

contrary to all evidence tourists
too have a life to leave behind
there are marks on their bodies
from the business where they hone their hours

beneath this cannibal sun
they tan their civilized souls
in the swell's decibels
their anxieties grow deaf

but the dustcloud stirs up wing dreams
essences foam
drip in between the appearances

in the end they survive the pleasure
return to their affairs
                        their sandcastles

MANACA IZNAGA

en la memoria zurda
                              todo una sola vez
como un pomo repleto de cocuyos
si nada fue futuro nada será pasado

con rocío en la prisa
                              espigas en el alma
esa torre torcida en chesterfield
tiene que ver contigo

                              también la torre eiffel
siempre al tanto de lo que no sucede
universal como la tojosita

el wye y el agabama
no líneas multiplicaciones puntos
sino la mancha hambrienta de sentido

MANACA IZNAGA

in southpaw memory
                              everything only once
like a jar full of cocuyos
if nothing was future nothing will be past

with dew in the urgency
                              sprigs in the soul
that twisted tower in chesterfield
has something to do with you

                              the eiffel tower too
always up to date about what's not going on
universal like a mourning dove

the wye and the agabama
no lines multiplications points
just the hungry stain of sense

CENTRAL FNTA

el sitio no es ameno
ni como estar ensimismado en ti
pastora de los cochinos del alma
el monte fue talado

y la leña quemada en las calderas
después el ingenio fue demolido
y nada huele a mieles iniciales
para colmo la fuente se secó

y la sed misma se fue a otra parte
las flores olvidaron su color
y se realizan solo en el mercado

todo el mundanal ruido se erizó
pastora de los enjambres del cuerpo
y el jilguero es realismo socialista

CENTRAL FTNA

the place is not pleasant
or like being self-absorbed in you either
shepherdess of soul pigs
the backwoods were felled

and the lumber burned in caldrons
after the sugar mill was destroyed
and nothing smells like starting point syrups
to top it off the fountain dried up

and even thirst went elsewhere
the flowers forgot their color
only realized in the market

all the worldly sound bristled
shepherdess of body swarms
and the goldfinch is socialist realism

AZOTEA DE REINA

incomodísimo
                    como barriga
tendera interior que corta el paso
tela olorosa a lluvia

este poema para resolver
escrito sin camisa e inconcluso
como edificio de microbrigada
anhelo desconchado

sus tablitas picadas de viruela
su plástico elocuente
este poema comido de hormigas

escrito al resplandor
como nunca
                    la realidad en obras

AZOTEA DE REINA

so awkward
                like a big gut
inside clothesline cutting me off
fabric fragrant with rain

this poem just to get by
written shirtless and unfinished
like a microbrigade building
longing chipped-away

its boards rough with smallpox
its eloquent plastic
this poem run through with ants

written under the sun's glare
like never before
                reality under construction

CALLE GALEANO

la lluvia borra los garabatos de la luz
sobre las tensas ruinas
el son que te apañaron
se enreda con los hilos de la sed

un revuelo sin alas ambarino
hace a todos dudar
menos al tipo calvo que se inunda
sin ganas de apurarse

aunque nadie lo note la ciudad se deslíe
bajo el civil aguacero de mayo
un azúcar febril

te cuartea los labios cuando silbas
el sitio equivocado
donde solo el instante persevera

CALLE GALEANO

the rain erases the scrawls of light
on tense ruins
the song they stole from you
gets tangled in the silk threads

a wingless amber fluttering
makes everyone doubt
except the bald guy sinking
with no desire to rush

even though nobody notices the city dissolves
beneath the civil may downpour
a feverish sugar

quarters your lips when you whistle
the wrong place
where only the instant endures

VALLE DE LOS INGENIOS

el paisaje no cuenta
hasta que aparece la palma real
nada dice el jagüey
tienta con sus raíces la calor

bajo un tronco de forma improvisada
se da la mejor sombra
templo de lagartijas hormiguero
el ave que no canta ni hace nido

mientras la palma se hinca de rodillas
para dejarte ver el fondo azul
el jagüey abraza para matar

creces entre los frutos más salobres
semillas como estrellas
alma la celulosa que se rumia

VALLE DE LOS INGENIOS

the landscape does not count
until a royal palm shows up
the jagüey tree says nothing
tempts the heat with its roots

beneath the trunk with a shape offhand
there is the best shade
temple of lizards anthill
the bird who doesn't sing or nest

while the palm kneels down
to let you see the blue background
the jagüey tree embraces to kill

you grow among the saltiest fruits
seeds like stars
soul the cellulose grazing on herself

CASILDA

y las olas en yunta
se tienden al tajo de la distancia
árboles del pasado
palma cana yagruma uva caleta

sacan chispas al viento
y la belleza hostiga
con su entrepierna oscura
caderas que bien pueden desollar

y los catamaranes
laten como relojes de pared
un bolígrafo sueco

se derrama en la arena tropical
nadie sabe qué hacer con el lagarto
sin piel en la canasta

CASILDA

and the waves yoked
stretch out on the edge of distance
trees from the past
sabal palm yagruma sea grape

they make the wind spark up
and beauty harasses
with its dark inner thigh
hips that can flay you

and the catamarans
pound like wall clocks
a swedish pen

spills on the tropical sand
nobody knows what to do with the lizard
skinless in the basket

EL RINCÓN

llegué donde quería minucioso
solo que no quería
                              ir a ninguna parte
mejor estar desempolvado aquí

donde tú siempre estás
                              al costado entrelíneas
como un soneto perpendicular
no te conozco pero sé quién eres

seguiría otro curso otra derrota
incluso rimaría
si dios mismo no fuera un desterrado

el panteón no se insulte
mas en esta agrafía su disnea
solo tengo fe en ti

EL RINCÓN

i got to where i wanted painstakingly
it's just that i didn't want
                            to go anywhere
better to be here dusted off

where you are always
                    at the edge between the lines
like a perpendicular sonnet
i don't know you but i know who you are

i would follow another course another wrong way
i would even rhyme
if god himself weren't banished

not to insult the pantheon
but in this agraphia its hunger for air
i only have faith in you

CALLE DESENGAÑO

es hora de volver a la materia
ingeniar otra forma
                    para los fieles átomos
es hora de ser pluma

de lechuza desprendida en la noche
o llama sin tres piedras
harina mineral en una güira
es hora de no ser

ese cuerpo cujeado por los años
volverse imprevisible
con imaginación y tres libras de más

es hora de hacer algo
                    para que el sueño siga
porque la vida no es la única forma de estar

CALLE DESENGAÑO

it is time to return to matter
come up with another way
                              for the faithful atoms
it is time to be owl

feather shed in the night
or flame without three stones
mineral flour in a calabash
it is time to not be

the body seasoned from the years
to become unpredictable
with imagination and three pounds too many

it is time to do something
                              so the dream keeps going
because life is not the only way of staying

PASEO DEL PRADO

este país se nos fue de los pies
y tomó otro camino
                        con su densa rutina
que ni una rumba puede alebrestar

mulatas legendarias
abanican la espera maduras de calor
y chinos hacen cola sonrientes
a las puertas de nada

país de reguetón doble moneda
estridencia ideológica
donde lo único decente es el sol

país alzado en ruinas triangulares
sin aire en la escalera
que ya no queda aquí ni regresa contigo

PASEO DEL PRADO

this country has gotten out of foot
it took another way
                            with its dense routine
not even a rumba could upset

legendary mulatas
fanning their wait ripe with heat
and chinos in line smile
at the doors of nothing

country of reggaetón dual currency
ideological stridency
where the only thing decent is the sun

country resolute in triangular ruins
breathless on the stairs
no longer here or returning with you

CASA DE ZENAIDA

resuelto a reparar lo irreparable
en la ciudad bloqueada por el polvo
la mesa convertida
                    en idea de mesa

la jicotea en concha vegetal
y las hojas carnosas con ribetes
en fósil acezante
                    le buscas un sentido

al solar atestado
a cada araña de la barbacoa
mas este espacio tiene su compás

ni la muerte se apura llega tarde
por un sitio decente
a sacudir el ser con un trapito

CASA DE ZENAIDA

resolved to repair what is irreparable
in the city blocked up by dust
table changed
                  to idea of table

turtle to vegetal shell
and leaves fleshy with trim
to panting fossil
                  you search for a meaning

to the packed tenement house
to every spider in the loft
still this space holds your rhythm

not even death is in a hurry gets here late
looking for a decent spot
to dust off being with a tiny rag

ACKNOWLEDGEMENTS

Earlier versions of some of these poems appear in the following: *The Punch Magazine, Tupelo Quarterly, The Kenyon Alumni Bulletin*, and *Hwaet! 20 Years of the Ledbury Poetry Festival.*

Our thanks to James Byrne for his tireless support of our work; to Aaron Kent and the editorial staff at Broken Sleep for their efforts; and to our family for their unwavering belief in what we do.

DI TU DESASOSIEGO

www.ingramcontent.com/pod-product-compliance
Lightning Source LLC
Chambersburg PA
CBHW032227080426
42735CB00008B/746